Immortalize Me

By

Xtina Marie

Xtina Marie

A HellBound Books LLC Publication
Copyright © 2020 by HellBound Books Publishing LLC
All Rights Reserved

Cover and art design by Luke Spooner

for
HellBound Books Publishing LLC

No part of this book may be reproduced, stored in a retrieval system, or transmitted by any means, electronic, mechanical, photocopying, recording or otherwise without written permission from the author
This book is a work of fiction. Names, characters, places and incidents are entirely fictitious or are used fictitiously and any resemblance to actual persons, living or dead, events or locales is purely coincidental.

www.hellboundbookspublishing.com

Printed in the United States of America

Acknowledgements

A very special shout out goes to my partner at HellBound Books Publishing LLC and co-host in the Panic Room, James H. Longmore. We're coming up on 200 episodes! Here's to 200 more!

Thank you again, to my badass cover artist, Luke Spooner.

A million and one thanks to Denise Jury for seeing the booboos that I can't!

To Rosemary O'Brien: Thank you for introducing me to free verse poetry that I actually loved! I'm proud to be a part of The Nu Romantics. Several of my poems were inspired by the daily prompts.

To my daughter, Hali: You are such a beautiful soul, thank you for being my best friend. Don't ever doubt how proud I am of you. And promise to call me often while you're backpacking across the world!

To my son, Shawn: You're metal AF. No, really. How many other 16 year olds have a favorite *Sabbath* song? You're growing into such an amazing young man. I can't wait to see the great things you accomplish. One day you'll remember how cool your mom is.

To Christian: Thank you. For giving me reason after reason to write happy poems. For making me see myself through your eyes. For making me laugh so much it hurts. For making me never want to play *Anywhere but Here* again. I love you madly.

Xtina Marie

Contents:

The Pull
Unreality
The Lucky Ones
Words
Magic
We Laugh
The Perfect Dad
Time
Bare Margins
To Make You Feel
Crave
Missing Out
Underneath
A Whole Lifetime
In Your Arms
Giant Pink Elephants
Two Evils
Paper Cuts
This
Warmth
Salt & Pepper Hairs
Smothered Moans
Carolyn
Johnny & Randy

Xtina Marie

Poeting
What's Left
Dance with Me
Damsel in Distress
Taste of Autumn
Summer Night
Dreams
I Can't Dance
Claim Me
The First Chapter
Vigorous Passion
Give Me Clouds
I Am Yours
Inspiring
Our Perfect Storm
As She'd Imagined
Forever
Bygone Tears
Free Me
Twisted Words
They Never Were
God Vacations
The Wind
Even Though
The Memory of You
Scribbled Words
The Empty Seat
In Your Cage

Outgrowing Christmas
Promise
Static
Familiar
Serenading
As One
Danger
The Meaning
Good Girl
As His
2 a.m.
A Mess
Savage
Forgotten Demons
Sit a Spell
Orphan
Silhouette
Chaos
Carolina Silverbells
Harsh Truths
He Kisses
Destiny
Terrible Driver
Escape You
The Smile
Put Me in My Place
Music Was Life
Immortalized

*If a writer falls in love with you,
you can never die.*
-Mik Everett

The Pull

We have this
pull.
This draw.
This connection.
More than want,
or desire
but a
crazy need,
crazy addiction
we can't
escape from.
Haunting,
compelling,
consuming
my every
thought.
When we kiss
I forget
where I end
and you begin.
When you take
a breath
I exhale.

Xtina Marie

Come
take my hand
and never fight
the pull.

Unreality

Scattered
shattered
thoughts fragment
confusion clouds
unreality
disjointed phrases
rattle
uselessly
unneeded
paranoia
spins 'round
and 'round
frightened, I
lash out
spew
hateful words
I'll forget
when I come
down
when I land
safely
once more
in unreality

Xtina Marie

The Lucky Ones

Is love
always
like this,
I wonder

then I
look
at you
and my heart
liquefies
pools
before you

and I know
we're
the lucky ones

we're
the ones
writers write
about
in epic

romance novels
song writers croon
about
in timeless
love songs
artists paint
when they're
fantasizing
about
the one

and I
don't wonder
anymore

I know

we're
the lucky ones

Xtina Marie

Words

I always
used
my words
to build you up
when you
felt small
to soothe you
when you
were hurting
to mend you
when you
felt broken
and

You let me

You always
used
your words
to punish
me
when you
were miserable
to hurt
me
when you

were in pain
to destroy
me
when you
were defeated
and

I let you

Xtina Marie

Magic

There's magic
in your touch
that I feel
every time
you are near

a buzzing
a tingling
starts
at the tips
of my fingers
travelling
the length
of me
leaving me
breathless
light-headed

my world
tilts
spins
and I
fall
into your arms

I fall

into
you

Xtina Marie

We Laugh

We laugh
often
your
full-bellied roars
and my
hysterical giggles
taken completely
in silliness
'til we are
struggling
for breath
not caring
who is watching
or if they
are judging
our
shenanigans
for we are
too busy
enjoying
each other
to notice

The Perfect Dad

My hazel eyes
so much
like my father's
stare in
the mirror,
hair hanging
limp
the ends
dripping
slowly
fresh-faced
from the
the shower
skin red
and raw
because
I still
feel unclean
no matter how hard
I try to scrub
away

Xtina Marie

the shame
of years
spent
pretending
you were
the perfect
dad

Time

Time flies
marches on
heals all
wounds
is of the
essence

blah blah

but
what is time,
really?

I watch
the sands
fall
soundlessly
ticking away
seconds
I'll never
recapture
no do overs
it's now
or never
no time
like the

Xtina Marie

present
take chances
make the
first move
say you're
sorry
ride the
fucking
roller coaster

do
something

anything

because
when you are
eighty
it's not gonna
matter
if he laughed
in your
face
who was
wrong
or if
you vomited
all over
the freckle-faced kid
sitting in the

seat in front
of you

do something

anything

and
do
it
now

Xtina Marie

Bare Margins

Where is
God
we ask
while
searching
fancy cathedrals &
sanctuaries
filled with
stuffy
men and women
who wouldn't
recognize
Jesus
if they
passed him
on the
street
too busy
worrying
whether the
expensive red clutch
matches the red
in the
King James Bible
while they
pretend

to take notes
but don't look
too closely
the margins are
bare

Xtina Marie

To Make You Feel

I yearn
to write
to create
something
beautiful
out of mere
words
give them
meaning
make them
more
than words

I yearn
to paint
vivid pictures
in your mind
so vivid
you can taste
the pineapple
as the juice
runs down
my chin
and see
the gooseflesh
on my arms
when I am

searching for
my favorite
blanket

I yearn
to make you
feel

Lost
in the
darkness
I found
guilt

Crave

You are
better than
the best drug
I've ever been
high on
the best buzz
I've ever been
drunk on
intense
consuming
so addicting
I crave
the next fix
before
I've come
down
from the last

Xtina Marie

Flying Through space (sub)

Missing Out

When I see
a book
any book
anywhere
I pause
try to make out
the cover,
title
author
wondering
if I am
missing out
on something
amazing

Xtina Marie

Underneath

My favorite
part
of wearing
lingerie
is the way
he slides
it off me
slowly
in anticipation
of the
creamy
skin
revealed
underneath

I want to be all that you'll ever need

Xtina Marie

A Whole Lifetime

Asleep
in the dark
the dead of night
no sounds
but the
white noise
the hum
of the fridge
snapping
to life

I reach for
you
feel your
warmth
as our fingers
lock together
a perfect fit
as the cool
of my cheek
meets the
warmth
of your chest
and I hear
the echo
of my heart beat

I know
I've lived
a whole lifetime
and it's only
in your arms
that I've ever
truly
been home

Xtina Marie

Homeless
a nomad
vagabond

In Your Arms

There is a
place
my mind used
to wander
when I was
young—
quiet
soothing
tranquil
serene

And I
thought
it was
magical
but fictional

Until

I woke up
in your
arms

Xtina Marie

Giant Pink Elephants

He holds my hand
as we stroll
around the
midway
past the
Haunted House
and the
Gypsy woman
trying to
guess my weight
and the vendors
with their
cotton candy,
funnel cake
and those
soft pretzels
everyone loves
and I
daydream
of the
next town
the next girl
who'll laugh
as her boyfriend

spends his
paycheck
hoping to win
that giant pink
elephant

Xtina Marie

Two Evils

When I was
a child
I was
haunted
by a
recurring
nightmare.

The dead of night,
an unfamiliar
long, winding
dirt road—
shoulders that
dropped off
into nothingness
so I walked
down the middle

'til
up ahead
I see headlights
distant
but coming closer.

With heart racing;
blood roaring
deafening

in the still night
I must decide
the lesser
of two
evils.

Xtina Marie

Paper Cuts

All over
my body
I have these
tiny
miniscule
barely there
paper cuts
they sting
especially
when it's hot
and beads
of sweat
glance
over them
you can't see
them
and I
doubt
you notice
me flinch
when my
t-shirt
catches one
but I
feel the
fresh blood
surface

when a new one
appears
every time
you
lie to me

Xtina Marie

This

There are
bills to be paid
and dishes
in the sink,
work is
neverending
and the dogs
need baths—

but here
we sit
on the porch
swinging lazily,
your arm
resting
along my back
watching the
grass grow
because
this

this
is
what's
important

Warmth

Submerged
in a warm
bath
the water
gently
rippling
around my
breasts,
my toes
play over the
faucet
wrinkled
and pruney

I think
the water has
cooled
but a
slight
flick of
my hand
is all that
is needed
to remind me
the water's
always
been warm

Xtina Marie

Thoughts
drift
to you—
a slight
flick of
my hand
if you will—
and I am
reminded
of your
warmth

Salt & Pepper Hairs

I just cleaned out
that sink—
scrubbed
'til I could see
my reflection
in the faucet,
and yet
I find here
a million tiny
salt & pepper
hairs—
a tell-tale sign
that you
shaved
this morning

Turning the water on
and grabbing a
washcloth
I ponder the
conversation
with my friend—
the one where
she complained

Xtina Marie

tirelessly
about this
very thing
with her husband

And I smile
hoping I'll be
cleaning this
same sink
when all of the
black hairs
have turned
white

I fall in love
With you
More
Everyday

Xtina Marie

Smothered Moans

He smothers
my moans
with his
kisses,
his tongue
darting
over mine,
his eyes
zoned in on
the flutter
of my lashes
and the
ecstasy
dancing
across
my face
as his
fingers
seek out
my warmth
and plunge
deep.

Writhing,

and starting to
sweat,
knees buckling
I climb
higher
and higher,
my smothered
moans
struggling
to become
screams
when
the fire
ignites
and the passion
washes
ever so
sweetly
over me

I wish
I could
afford
to buy you
your
heart' s desire

Carolyn

I invent lives
for the strangers
I pass,
nameless people
I glimpse
for only a
moment
while riding
along the
back roads
staring
out the window.

This one house
sits on a hill
overlooking
the winding
country road
and occasionally
I see her
out watering
her rose bushes
in a polka dotted
apron
with ruffles
for sleeves.

Xtina Marie

I like to
pretend
her name is
Carolyn,
and she's a
regular
at the
Baptist church
a few blocks
away.
She makes the best
lemonade and her
apple pie
took 2nd place
at the church
cake-walk
last year.

I wave
when the
weather is nice
and the top's down—
sometimes
she waves back.
Maybe one day
she'll invite me
to sit a spell
and we'll gossip
about Bethany
two houses down,

while we sip
lemonade

Xtina Marie

Johnny & Randy

When I
was a child
we played
out back
behind
Johnny and Randy's
house.
It was hot
in the shade
and I preferred
laying in
the cool grass
under the big oak tree
trying to make out
shapes in the
fluffy white clouds
while Randy
wanted to play
Cops and Robbers and
Cowboys and Indians.

Under that tree
Johnny grabbed my hand,
pointed at the sky
and told me
he saw a bunny

with whiskers
a mile long
and turned his head
to kiss my cheek
so fast
I wondered
if I'd imagined it.

Yet I can
still feel
the warmth
of his lips
when the
cool grass tickles
my bare legs
or I
spot a bunny
in the summer sky.

Xtina Marie

Poeting

"An artist
with no canvas
in which to create
is still an
artist.
For even without
a paintbrush
in hand
they are still
creating
their next masterpiece,"

I tell myself
as I stare
frustratedly
at the blank
piece of paper
before me
with nothing more
than a few doodles
here and there.

A poet
is still
a poet
even when she
is not poeting.

What's Left

What's left
when the
newness
has worn off
and things
aren't shiny
like they once
were?
When the
little things
stop being
important
and everyday life
settles in…
When I
fall asleep during
your favorite
movie
and my
cooking skills
resemble
Rachel Green's
instead of
Rachel Ray's…

What's left
is sitting side by side

Xtina Marie

on the porch
holding hands
in the summer sun
taking time
out of the day
to watch
the grass grow,
holiday dinners
with the kids
and movie marathons
when it's rainy,
late night talks
in bed
with your head
cradled to my chest
after a long day

and laughter.

Perfect

When I was
a young girl
dreaming
of happiness
and trying
so very
desperately
to escape
my reality—
the painful
existence
I bore—
I'd lie awake
and play
"Anywhere but here."

I'd daydream
of life
and paint
pictures
in my mind

The perfect
love
the perfect
home
the perfect

Xtina Marie

life

Never realizing
how unrealistic
and subjective
"Perfect"
was

Older, wiser now
I know there is
so much
more than
"Perfect"

And I
never
ever
close my eyes
and play
that childhood
game

For in
your arms
I am
exactly
unequivocally
completely
right where
I want to be

Stop
and smell
the roses
with me

Xtina Marie

Dance with Me

Dance with me
barefoot
at midnight,
classic rock
on the radio
while we laugh
every time I
step on your toes,
my head pressed
to your chest
so I can hear
your heart
beating

Dance with me
on the porch
in the spring
at twilight
to the music
of the crickets,
the fireflies
flitting
over the yard
while I inhale
a deep breath
of you
Dance with me

I promised him
a mad love.
Beautiful
sweet
and simple.

Damsel in Distress

No damsel
in distress
as he'd
often called her,
she wasn't crying
"help me, help me"
or "save me, save me"
as he'd ridiculed,
and when she'd tired
of his bullshit
she only paused
briefly
before stepping over
the damaged man
he'd become...

Taste of Autumn

Taste the sweet chill
of autumn
as the yellows
fade to orange
and the
fire burns bright,
dripping honey
like salted rain
from my lips

Xtina Marie

Summer Night

Riding with the
top down
on a summer night,
messy hair
escaping
my bun,
stinging
the sides of
my face,
our fingers
entwined
on the gear shift,
we brake
at a red light,
lifting our hands
to your mouth
you kiss
my fingers,
I watch the reflection
in your eyes—
light changing—
red to green
and without a word
our hands fall
back to the shifter,
as everything around us
becomes a blur.

Dreams

never forget
youthful dreams
of
talking,
connecting,
long, slow kissing
and
everlasting love

Xtina Marie

I Can't Dance

Sometimes
we forget
the little things—
saying I love you,
or asking how
the day was,
neglecting to
kiss goodnight,
talking 'til
the sun comes up
or laughing
together
often.

Always
always
stop
whatever
you are doing
to dance
barefoot
with me
in the kitchen
even though
we both know
I can't dance.

Claim Me

I'm reminded
of your touch
as I
gingerly
lower myself
into the chair,
my ass still
tender
from the
paddle, the crop,
your hand

I smile at the pain
and run my
fingers
over the
marks
left behind
from the rope
you used
to restrain me

I love the way
you
claim me

Xtina Marie

The First Chapter

A lifetime ago
we held hands
for the first time
at the library
among the
dusty shelves,
the smell
of old books
and adventures
mingling with
the hope of
new romance
tightening my
tummy

A glance,
a light hand
grazing
your thigh
not so innocently
and flirty,
whispered words
began
our first chapter

Vigorous Passion

You bask
in my pheromones
fingers
poetry on my skin
lips part
on a sigh
as you
thrust
into my heat
love sings
the vigorous
passion

Xtina Marie

Give Me Clouds

Give me a
cloudy day over
the sun shining
bright,
and a chill in
the air
over the warmth

I want the sting
of the crisp
mountain breeze
dancing across
my face
rather than sand
between my toes

And before
spending money on
fancy symphony tickets,
turn the radio to
classic rock,
grab a blanket and
meet me in the backyard

I Am Yours

I love
the marks
I find
scattered
about my body
in the morning—
the red, raised skin
on my wrists
from the rope
you tied securely,
the bruising
here and there
from your
possessive kisses
and nibbles
in sensitive places,
the welts covering
my ass
reminding me
often
just who
I belong to.

I am yours

Xtina Marie

Inspiring

our bodies
meeting
in slow desire—
a beautiful merging,
a sensual seduction
inspiring
the poets and musicians
to make
tantalizing tension

Our Perfect Storm

Kiss me
sweetly
on the lips,
look into my
eyes
and whisper
how much you
adore me,
take me to
the edge
with just the
touch of
your hand
gliding
along my flesh
like a soft
summer breeze
moments before
grabbing my hair
roughly
growling
into my ear:
You're mine
as you

Xtina Marie

slam into me,
animalistic
noises escaping
your throat
playing
across my face,
sweat dripping
from your
drenched body
like the sprinkles
at the beginning of a
summer rain shower
moments before
we erupt in
thunderous magic,
holding
onto each other
in the aftermath
of our
perfect storm

As She'd Imagined

together
strolling
hand in hand
unhurried
exactly
as she had
imagined

Xtina Marie

Forever

I can see
the future
when I look
into your eyes;
the same
hazel
that stares
back at me now
with a few extra
lines etched
at the corners,
the same wink
that still gives me
butterflies,
older, wiser—
the salt and pepper
has turned
to white
but still decorates
that jawline
I can never
stop staring at.
I don't need
a psychic
or crystal ball
because
I can see

forever
in your eyes

Xtina Marie

Bygone Tears

fleeting dreams
of bygone tears,
a memory and
melancholy clouds
caress my lips
in the heat
of salty rain

Free Me

Paint my
skin in
reds and purples
while you
free me
from the
demons
I hold onto unaware
'til I'm
writhing
in pain,
in ecstasy,
in submission—
the stress
of the world
dissipates
melts
dissolves
with the tears
that slide
soundlessly
from my eyes
to stain the
pillow

Xtina Marie

Twisted Words

I'll write
twisted words
hard just like
broken hopes
and awful cries

They Never Were

Leaves of
yellow, orange, brown
twirl and dance
on the air
falling discarded
while grey skies
loom somber and still
threatening
to open up, let loose
and purge us from
the sins of summer
so quickly forgotten
almost as if
they never were

Xtina Marie

God Vacations

I think
God
vacations
in the
mountains
of Tennessee,
painting
the sky
during fall—
blues, purples
and pinks—
while sitting
on a porch
overlooking
the water
surrounded by the
yellows and browns
and orange leaves
of the
changing
trees,
the breeze
ruffling
perfect hair.
I think
when God
isn't in

Heaven
He's perfectly
content
to rest his hat
in Tennessee.

Xtina Marie

The Wind

The wind
whispers
through
skeletal leaves
as gray clouds
twist in the
brisk chill

Even Though

I want
to build
snowmen
and have
snowball fights
even though
I always
complain
my hands
are freezing

I want to
snuggle
on the couch
in flannel
sipping
hot cider,
watching
our favorite
movies
even though
I always
end up
falling asleep

I want
to lie in bed

Xtina Marie

'til noon
on Saturday
listening to the
quiet
of the snow
falling
pulling you
back under
the comforter
with me
even though
I know
we have
things to do

I love that
you love my
"even though"

cast your gaze
to our hands—
fingers touch—
a whisper
of a promise
lingers

Xtina Marie

The Memory of You

cold lips
linger,
wine
burning
heat
as I
hold the
memory
of you
deep into
the night

Scribbled Words

a notebook
scribbled words
become
deep feelings
excitement perhaps?
maybe fear
of the
unknown

Xtina Marie

The Empty Seat

I sat
in the cold
on our bench
and waited
fingers
growing numb
in fur-lined
gloves
remembering
the warmth
of your kisses
the comfort
of your embrace
while the snow
danced
landing in wet
clumps
on the empty seat
beside me

In Your Cage

I am nothing
but
a
bird
in your cage—
in this
cage

I am trapped
confined
held captive
imprisoned

By your love—
you say
you love me
unconditionally
wholly
completely
and
I want
to be loved

So I do
nothing but
occasionally
flutter my

Xtina Marie

wings
against the
bars
of my cage
and wait

For the love
that you
promised

Outgrowing Christmas

Like a child
I stare
transfixed
at the sparkle
of the tree;
shiny bulbs
fancy ornaments
an Angel
perched atop
and I wait
with anticipation
but not for
Old St Nick,
instead
I wait
for the
smile
on his face
as he
tears
at the colorful
wrapping
taking time to
shake the box

Xtina Marie

and try to guess
what's inside.
No matter
how old I am
I will
never
outgrow
Christmas

Promise

adventure
fresh
new beginning
we leave
the same old
and
together
we kiss
the unknown
wild and free
with promise

Xtina Marie

Static

Kiss me
breathless
at the
grocery store
in the middle
of the
aisle—
your hand
tangled
in my hair
and
your tongue
swirling
around mine—
while
old women
stop and stare,
frowning
at our display
and young girls
blush at
our passion
but not a care
we have
for everything
around us
is just

static,
background noise
to our story

Xtina Marie

Familiar

listen
to the
familiar
magick
of the
storm—
feel it
kiss the
earth,
an erotic
desire
the Goddess
weaves

Serenading

we dance
to the music
of our love,
soft cellos
and violins
serenading
as your hand
glides over
the small of
my back
and you lead me
under the stars
and through
the grass
on the dance floor
of our dreams

Xtina Marie

As One

Two hearts
become
one
beat
as one
bleed
as one

through
life's
struggles
and life's
joys

the ups
and downs
the good
and bad

from the
first chapter
until the
last
I'll stand
by your
side
hand in hand

our two hearts
have become
one
beat
as one
bleed
as one

Xtina Marie

Danger

seduce me
with your danger,
rough stubble
teasing the grin
as you
sigh
into your
whiskey,
your hand
trailing over
the nylon of my
black stockings

The Meaning

It's about
the noise
of video games
and warring music,
the click clack
of dog claws
on hardwood
and chaos of
multiple voices
all vying
for the same
attention,
the clutter and mess
from the
pancake brunch
on Sunday
and the sneakers
that are
never lined up
by the door,
it's the laughter
on Saturday night,
playing board games
and watching movies,
it's the pillow talk
when the house
is quiet

Xtina Marie

and the heat
of your body
against mine,
your arms
safe and warm
as I drift off
to sleep—
and knowing
I get to do it
over and over

Good Girl

I crave
pain
to satisfy
the need
spank me
control me
make me behave
I'll be your
good girl

Xtina Marie

As His

he stalks me
with his mind
brings me
to the brink
over and over
with those
eyes
that see
every part of me

he tastes me
with his mouth
that tongue
that trails
my curves
and every inch
as he exposes
more and more
of the body he's
claimed as his

2 a.m.

I love 2 a.m.
when
the house
is quiet
and the bed
is warm,
where we
talk
about our day—
your hand
absently
rubbing
the side of
my breast—
a trace of
mint
from your
toothpaste
wafting
toward me.
I love 2 a.m.
when the phone
isn't ringing,
and the dogs
aren't barking,
the kids are
asleep

Xtina Marie

and no one
needs me
at work,
when I am
no one…
but yours

A Mess

Dance in
the dark
where no one
can see if
you've got the
moves just right,
your toes
point perfectly
and your hair
is a mess

Xtina Marie

Savage

I hunger,
starving
for your skin
as I hunt
for your mouth
like a
savage

Forgotten Demons

Lost
in thought
I stare off
reflecting
on some
unseen
forgotten
demon
my mind
likes to
hold onto
and I prod
at him
silent
until I can
convince myself
he's not really
my enemy
but my
friend

Xtina Marie

Sit a Spell

let's sit a spell
under
our favorite tree
and laugh
with me
every chance
we get
enjoying
each moment
as if
we've not a care
in the world

Orphan

I had the dream again
the one where
you were here
with me still
and I didn't feel
so lost
so alone
in this
vast world
but then I awoke
and I was again
an orphan

Xtina Marie

Silhouette

I explore
his silhouette
with nothing
but my eyes
slowly
making time
speak

Pull the
blinds
and lock the
doors
all I need
and ever will
is in your
arms

Xtina Marie

Chaos

Every man
for
himself and
survival
of the
fittest,
in the face of
danger
alarm
calamity
neighbors
stop waving
and eye you
warily
suddenly
wondering
if you're
friend or foe
chaos ensues

exactly

as

they'd

planned

Carolina Silverbells

The smell
of spring
is in
the air
wafting
towards us
sprinkled
in the bell-shaped
flowers of the
Carolina Silverbells
blowing
from the trees
to settle
soundlessly
at my
bare feet

a healthy love
nourishes
sufficiently

Harsh Truths

Fear of the
unknown
multiplies
discord,
disharmony,
hostility
allowing mayhem
to rule,
take over,
dominate
our minds—
focus instead on
the beauty
that surrounds
us daily;
the rain
falling
to the ground
washing away
the ugliness
of yesterday
allowing the
blooming flowers
to emerge—
the toothless
smile
of that baby

Xtina Marie

who knows not yet
of the woes
to come
innocent and trusting
peering at us
with eyes
unblemished by
harsh truths—
the wagging tail
from your neighbor's
noisy dog
the same one
who barks at 2 a.m.
disturbing
your precious slumber—
our society
is spoiled,
pampered,
coddled
and we've
forgotten
the real meaning
of life is
how we
live it

He Kisses

He kisses
the back of
my neck
and elicits
small moans
as the
pleasure
pulses through
my insides

I question
words
worn by
loose
lips

Destiny

sometimes
destiny
 reveals
sweet things
like
lovers
working
constantly
to make
the wind still
and the
hurricane
turn

Xtina Marie

Terrible Driver

I don't even mind
admitting
I'm a
terrible driver—
my mind
drifts
and my eyes
stray
to the gorgeous
trees
lining the streets,
the vivid blossoms
that bloom
in the spring—
reds and pinks
blues and purples—
or the skeletal
branches
brittle and frail
reaching out with
bony fingers
as the final leaves
float soundlessly
in the fall
to line the streets—
the same streets
I find it

difficult
to keep
my eyes on

Xtina Marie

every desire
knows
sweet pleasure
before
a gentle
death

Escape You

I always
seem
to end up
here
no matter
the years
that've passed
or the tears
I've shed,
the forgiveness
I'm told
is for me
and not you—
sometimes
unintentionally
I wander back
and for the
rest of the day
I'm trapped
hurting
cold and numb
unloved
abused,
seemingly
for your pleasure
and I have to
struggle

Xtina Marie

to escape you
all over
again

The Smile

you're liquor,
sweet on my
tongue
always better
just like
the smile

Xtina Marie

Put Me in My Place

Is it still
considered
topping
from the bottom
if I'm sassy
when I need
a good
flogging
or your hand
heating up
my ass,
coloring it
red and blue
and black?

When I'm
surly and snarky,
mouthy even
feeling
neglected, unused
if you've left
my skin
unmarked
for too long?

Or do I
just like it
when you need to
punish me
control me
dominate me
and put me
in my place?

Xtina Marie

Music Was Life

When I was
young
music was
life
and my
dreams
were filled
with you and
a kiss

Immortalized

I lay my words
before you,
these stolen
moments
I've chosen to
preserve,
little snippets
of me
immortalized
forever,
secret thoughts,
flitting desires
and lingering demons

Xtina Marie

About the Author

The Short Version:

Book Publisher, Poet, Podcaster, Writer, Mom, Bibliophile…

The Accidental Poet:

Xtina Marie is an avid horror and fiction genre reader, who became a blogger; who became a published poet; who became an editor; who now is a book publisher and CEO of Hell Bound Books Publishing with her co-host on The Panic Room Radio Show, James H. Longmore.

Her first book of poetry, Dark Musings has received outstanding reviews. It is likely Xtina was born to this calling. Writing elaborate twisted tales to entertain her classmates in middle school would later lead Xtina to use her poetry as a private emotional outlet in adult life—words she was hesitant to share publicly—but the more she shared, the more accolades her writing received.

She has two additional poetic narrative editions, Light Musings and Darkest Sunlight, a combination of both light and dark poetry. In 2018, Xtina fell in love with free verse, and began writing Without the Confines of My Rhymes, which was released in 2019.

Xtina has contributed works to the following:
Suite 269 by Christine Zolendz
Busted Lip: An Anthology
Monsters of Metal: An Anthology
The Intermission, Gore Carnival Book 2
A Lovely Darkness: Poetry with Heart
Black Candy: A Halloween Anthology of Horror
Collected Christmas Horror Shorts by Kevin J. Kennedy
Slashing Through the Snow: A Christmas Horror Anthology
Depraved Desires: Volume 1
Beautiful Tragedies
Damsels of Distress
Pieces of Us: A Collection of Flash Fiction, Short Stories, and Poetry

Subliminal Messages: A Collection of Poetry, Prose, and Quotes
Leaves of the Poet Tree by Andrew Aitken
Apocalypse of the Heart by Leah Negron and friends
Poetry Friends in Rhythm & Rhyme by Leah Negron
Graveyard Girls by Gerri R. Gray
Further Within Darkness & Light: A Collection of Poetry by Paul B Morris
The Light Shines Through: Anthology of Poetry
Paper Cuts

Xtina resides in the beautiful state of Tennessee, with her family and three yapping ankle biters.

You can find Xtina:
http://www.hellboundbookspublishing.com/index.html
https://www.facebook.com/XtinaMarie4031/
https://www.facebook.com/ThePanicRoomRadioShow/
https://www.amazon.com/Xtina-Marie/e/B01E1QNI3O?ref=sr_ntt_srch_lnk_1&qid=1589142288&sr=8-1

Xtina Marie

OTHER POETRY FROM HELLBOUND BOOKS

www.hellboundbookspublishing.com

Without the Confines of my Rhymes

Poetry is a beautiful thing, illustrating thoughts and emotions with concise, well-chosen words. A lot of poetry rhymes, adding additional flavor to the words, giving them a sense of rhythm, of flow

But what happens when you take away the rhyming, when you cast off the forms of convention and good sense?

Then the interesting things begin to come out. When the next line doesn't need to rhyme, anything can come next. As it is within the poems themselves, so it is with this book in its entirety.

Casting off the rhyming styles she used before, Xtina Marie embarks on a journey of emotional ups and downs, reflecting on love, loss, children and art.

So settle in, put on your wine-colored glasses, and take a trip without the confines of rhymes.

Darkest Sunlight

"The heart was made to be broken." - *Oscar Wilde*

To allow your heart to soar, you must risk the depths. Darkest Sunlight is the third poetic narrative from Xtina Marie. In this journey, readers will begin in the darkest of places yet revealed to us by this critically acclaimed poet, only to then find themselves thrust into the brightness of love before their eyes and minds can fully adjust. It is this shocking contrast which best conveys what it is to love, lose, and love again.

In Dark Musings, Xtina explored sadness. In Light Musings, she explored the intricacies of a loving heart. In Darkest Sunlight, Xtina Marie compares the opposite ends of the spectrum, and in doing so, she found a place darker than black.

<u>Dark Musings</u>

The perfect companion piece to Light Musings – The dark side of Xtina Marie's poetry delves into intense emotions: heartache, loss, hurt, pain, rage, and a dangerous consuming love which can drive one insane. Dark Musings is not a collection!

The author returned to the centuries old practice of Narrative Poetry—the telling of a story through poetry. If you believe you are brave enough to explore the savage emotions of the human heart; Dark Musings will test your mettle.

Light Musings

The perfect companion piece to Dark Musings – an intriguing mirror image of the darkness you have just read, but no less deep and soul stirring.

What a web she weaves. Light Musings is a poetic narrative—a story told through related poems. Xtina Marie is a master of this style. Known by her fans as the Dark Poet Princess, this term of endearment came about as a result of the horror genre embracing her first book: Dark Musings which continues to garner stellar reviews. Light Musings will not disappoint her loyal fans as darkness is present within these pages as well. However, this latest book will show a much larger audience that Xtina's poetry pulls out every feeling the reader has ever experienced—forcing them to feel with her protagonist. Light Musings shows us that love is made from darkness and light; something Xtina Marie explores like no one else.

Visceral Vices

Alexandrines singing of carnage, collapse, a capricious, convulsing wormwood bitterness reeking of decay, dolor, and delusions.

Sonnets hissing with treachery, tragedy, a trickling, liminal longing that cannot-and will never-be fulfilled.

Stories, alive with guttural shrieks and lilts, breeding demonic aura, human vengeance, and beasts and monsters that, like insoluble echoes or silhouetted revenants, are revived from pluperfect myths, modern inventions, and even spectral, Plutonian remembrances, never to be banished.
And, brewing in the cascades of blood and bones, much, much more.

Comprising 45 poems and 7 short stories, both previously published and new work, Visceral Vices is the author's first solo collection, embroidered with leaden barbs, laced with miasmic poisons, and, snaking across corpse-filled fissures, mortally taut in suspension with the surreal, gnarled, writhing skeins of fermenting fancies, plaguing aches, and gratuitous murder.

<u>Gray Skies of Dismal Dreams</u>

Prepare for an excursion into a gloomy world of shadows, where the days are never sunlit and blithe, and where the nights are wrapped in endless nightmares.

No happy endings or silver linings are found in the clouds that fill these gray skies.

But what you will find, gathered in one volume, are the darkest of poems and tales of horror, waiting to take your mind on a journey into realms of the uncheerful and the unholy.

An amazingly surreal collection of short stories and the darkest of poetry, all interspersed with stunning graveyard photographs taken by the multitalented author herself - an absolute must for every bookshelf!

Beautiful Tragedies

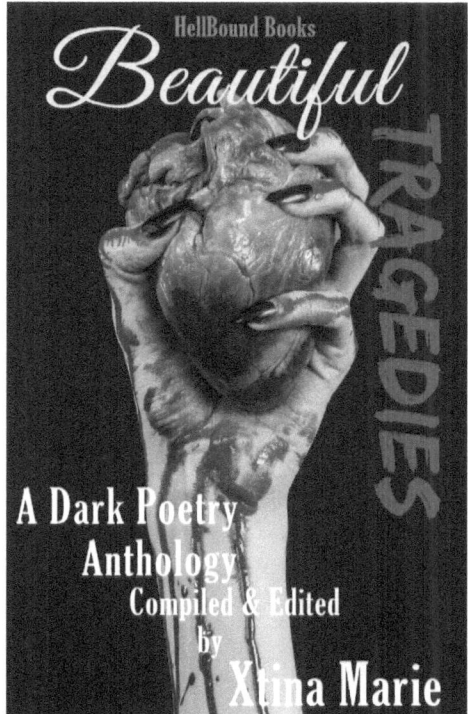

Only through dark poetry can a tragedy become something truly beautiful.

"Beauty is in the eye of the beholder." This phrase has origins dating back to ancient Greece, circa 300 BC; proving that some humans have always had the ability to see beauty where others could not.

Beautiful Tragedies is a compilation of 140 works by no less than fifty-five amazing poets writing in a variety of forms--all inspired by feelings born in the darkest of times.

Detours and Dead Ends

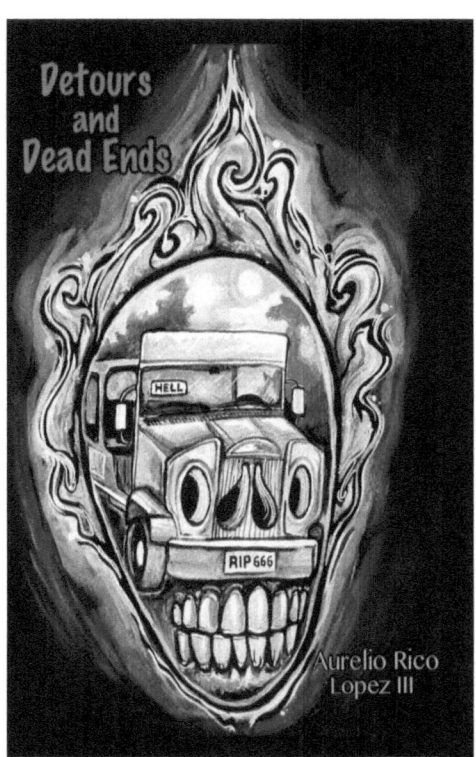

There are so many poems that invoke feelings of romance, wonderment, and joy.

These aren't them.

Aurelio Rico Lopez III is an exceedingly talented writer and poet who manages to conjure up scenes of mayhem, fear, and cosmic dread in this poetry collection, Detours and Dead Ends.

Lopez brings a bit of artistic flare to his signature style of writing and provides a book that takes the reader from murder to revenge, from unfortunate circumstances to several different flavors of the apocalypse.

So crack it open and enjoy the ride..

Tripping Balls

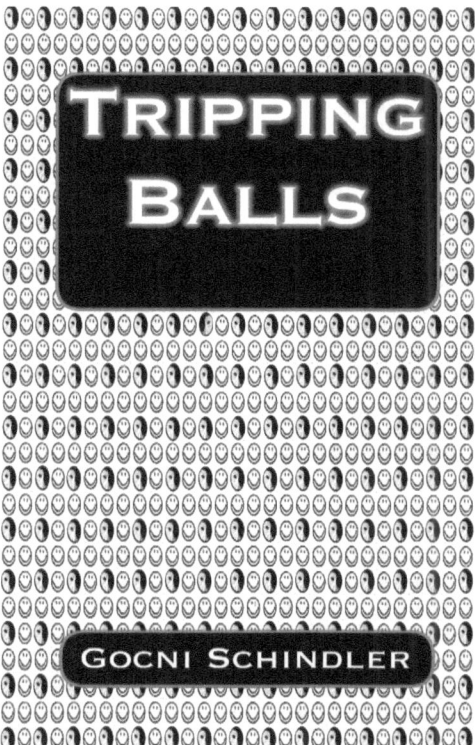

A thought provoking, eclectic, disturbing and at times downright weird collection of poetry, short stories and insightful musings from the inimitable Gocni Schindler....

He offers a variety of stories, which beautifully gives the awesome reader, like you, the opportunity to experience different levels of thought and contemplation. I know, it's so exciting! God willing, some humor as well.

A HellBound Books LLC Publication

www.hellboundbookspublishing.com

Printed in the United States of America

www.ingramcontent.com/pod-product-compliance
Lightning Source LLC
Chambersburg PA
CBHW030153100526
44592CB00009B/253